Fur

Cassie Mayer

Heinemann Library
Chicago, Illinois

Customer Service 888-454-2279

Visit our website at www.heinemannlibrary.com

Photo research by Tracy Cummins and Erica Newbery
Designed by Jo Hinton-Malivoire
Printed and bound in China by South China Printing Company
10 09 08 07 06
10 9 8 7 6 5 4 3 2 1

Library of Congress Cataloging-in-Publication Data

Mayer, Cassie.
Fur / Cassie Mayer.-- 1st ed.
    p. cm. -- (Body coverings)
Includes bibliographical references and index.
ISBN 1-4034-8371-X (hc) -- ISBN 1-4034-8377-9 (pb)
1. Fur--Juvenile literature. I. Title. II. Series.
QL942.M37 2006
573.5'8--dc22

2005035407

Acknowledgments

The author and publisher are grateful to the following for permission to reproduce copyright material:
Corbis pp. **4** (rhino, Royalty Free), **6** (Paul A. Souders), **11** and **12** (Nigel J. Dennis/Gallo Images), **15** and **16** (Kevin Schafer/zeta), **18** (Martin Harvey), **20** (Kevin Dodge), **22** (cat, Pat Doyle), **23** (porcupine, Nigel J. Dennis/Gallo Images); Flpa p. **22** (wild boar); Getty Images pp. **7** and **8** (Warden), **9**, **10** and **23** (sheep, Miller), **13** (Jones), **14** (Wolfe); Getty Images/Digital Vision pp. **4** (kingfisher), **5** (cheetah), **23** (cheetah); Getty Images/PhotoDisc pp. **4** (snail and lizard), **17**, **23** (giraffe); Nature Picture Library p. **22** (lion, Christophe Courteau).

Cover photograph of tiger fur, reproduced with permission of William Dow/Corbis. Back cover image of bear fur reproduced with permission of Warden/Getty Images.

Special thanks to the Smithsonian Institution and Jonathan Ballou for their help with this project.

Every effort has been made to contact copyright holders of any material reproduced in this book. Any omissions will be rectified in subsequent printings if notice is given to the publisher.

Contents

Animals have body coverings.
Body coverings protect animals.

feathers

scales

shell

skin

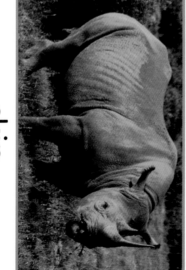

fur

Fur is a body covering.
Some animals have fur.

There are different types of fur.

Fur can be thick and straight.
What animal is this?

This animal is a bear.
Its fur keeps it warm.

Fur can be thick and curly.
What animal is this?

This animal is a sheep.
Its fur is called wool.

Fur can be sharp and pointy.
What animal is this?

This animal is a porcupine.
Its quills protect it from danger.

quills

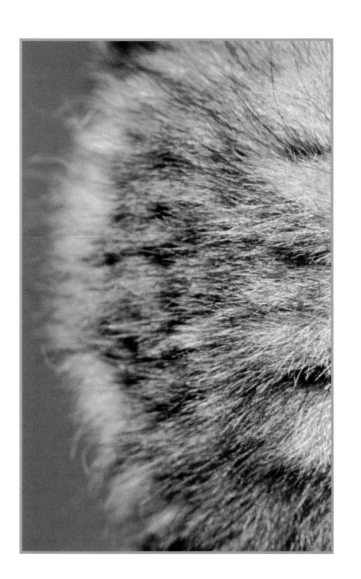

Fur can be soft and fluffy.
What animal is this?

baby cheetah

This animal is a baby cheetah.
Its fur changes when it grows.

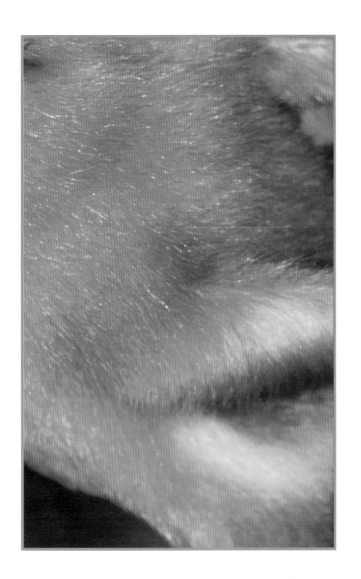

Fur can be bright colors.
What animal is this?

This animal is a tamarin.
Its fur is bright like the sun.

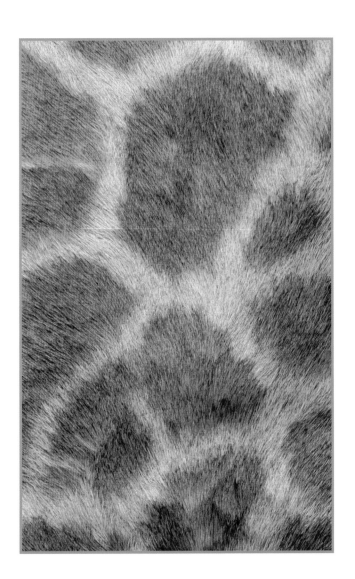

Fur can have patterns.
What animal is this?

This animal is a giraffe.
Its fur helps it hide.

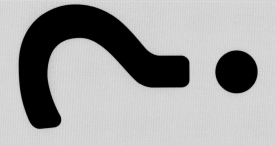

Do you have fur?

Yes, you have fur!
Your fur is called hair.

What is your fur like?

Fun Fur Facts

Sometimes fur stands up straight when animals are upset.

A lion's mane helps the lion look important.

Wild boars have fur that protects them from mud.

Picture Glossary

fur a type of body covering that many animals have

pattern a shape or color that repeats over and over again. Patterns help some animals hide.

quill a sharp and thick hair that protects porcupines

wool thick, curly fur that covers sheep

Index

Note to Parents and Teachers

In this book, children explore characteristics of fur and are introduced to a variety of animals that use this covering for protection. Visual clues and the repetitive question, "What animal is this?" engage children by providing a predictable structure from which to learn new information. The text has been chosen with the advice of a literacy expert to enable beginning readers success while reading independently or with moderate support. Scientists were consulted to provide both interesting and accurate content.

The book ends with an open-ended question that asks children to relate the material to their lives. Use this question as a writing or discussion prompt to encourage creative thinking and assess comprehension. You can also support children's nonfiction literacy skills by helping them to use the table of contents, picture glossary, and index.